WE THE PEOPLE

Pearl Harbor

by Andrew Santella

Content Advisers: Daniel Martinez, Historian, and
Thomas Shaw, President, USS *Arizona* Memorial Museum Association,
Honolulu, Hawaii

Reading Adviser: Rosemary G. Palmer, Ph.D.,
Department of Literacy, College of Education,
Boise State University

COMPASS POINT BOOKS
MINNEAPOLIS, MINNESOTA

Compass Point Books
3109 West 50th Street, #115
Minneapolis, MN 55410

Visit Compass Point Books on the Internet at *www.compasspointbooks.com*
or e-mail your request to *custserv@compasspointbooks.com*

On the cover: The battleships USS *West Virginia* and *Tennessee* sit low in the water
and burn after the Japanese surprise attack on Pearl Harbor on December 7, 1941.

Photographs ©: Bettmann/Corbis, cover, 4, 16, 19, 23, 34, 39; Defense Visual Information Center,
6, 9; Library of Congress, 7, 13, 30, 37; Franklin D. Roosevelt Library, 8, 27; Hulton/ Archive by
Getty Images, 10, 11, 15, 17, 20, 21, 24, 29, 31, 33, 35, 36, 38, 40; Defense Visual Information
Center/H.S. Wong, 12; Thomas D. Mcavoy/Time Life Pictures/Getty Images, 14; U.S. Navy/Time
Life Pictures/Getty Images, 18; Hulton-Deutsch Collection/Corbis, 22; AFP/Getty Images, 26;
Ronen Zilberman/Getty Images, 41.

Creative Director: Terri Foley
Managing Editor: Catherine Neitge
Photo Researcher: Marcie C. Spence
Designer/Page production: Bradfordesign, Inc./Jaime Martens
Cartographer: XNR Productions, Inc.

Library of Congress Cataloging-in-Publication Data
Santella, Andrew.
  Pearl Harbor / by Andrew Santella.
      p. cm. — (We the people)
Includes bibliographical references and index.
  ISBN 0-7565-0680-8
1. Pearl Harbor (Hawaii), Attack on, 1941—Juvenile literature. [1.Pearl Harbor (Hawaii)
Attack on, 1941. 2. World War, 1939-1945—Causes.] I. Title. II. We the people (Series)
(Compass Point Books)
D767.92.S3414 2004
940.54'26693—dc22   2003024190

TABLE OF CONTENTS

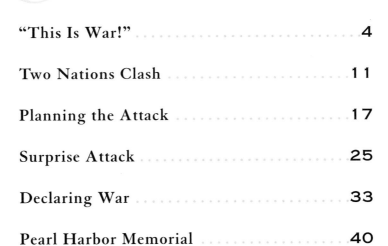

NOTE: *In this book, words that are defined in the glossary are in* **bold** *the first time they appear in the text.*

"THIS IS WAR!"

It was a quiet Sunday morning in Hawaii. All across the Hawaiian island of Oahu, people were just waking up. On the southern shore of Oahu were the ships of the United States Pacific Fleet, based at Pearl Harbor. Sailors on the ships were just beginning what they thought would be another ordinary Sunday.

Aboard one of the Navy's biggest ships was an officer named George Macartney Hunter. He was part of the crew of about 2,000 sailors who lived and worked on the

The giant guns of the USS Arizona, *which served from 1916 to 1941*

USS *West Virginia.* The *West Virginia* was one of seven American **battleships** that floated on "Battleship Row" in Pearl Harbor. It was 1941, and much of the world was at war. As the sun rose over Oahu on this December 7, however, the United States had not yet entered the fighting in Europe or Asia.

This was supposed to be a day of fun for Hunter and his crewmates. He had planned to play golf with three of his fellow officers. At 7:54 in the morning, though, alarm bells began ringing aboard the *West Virginia.* Hunter was not too concerned about the alarms. They often sounded for no reason and turned out to be false alarms. This time, however, the alarms rang a second time. Then, suddenly, an explosion shook the great ship. Hunter and some of his fellow officers looked at each other, and one of them cried, "This is war!" All of them raced to their stations.

Hunter made his way to one of the ship's decks, where he saw an awful scene. Ships in the harbor were burning, sending thick black smoke up toward the sky.

The USS West Virginia *on fire the morning of December 7, 1941*

On deck, sailors rushed about to get to their posts or save shipmates who were trapped by fire or rising water. Overhead, bomber planes flew in perfect formations of five planes each. On each wing of the planes was the image of a rising sun, the symbol of the empire of Japan.

*The Japanese hit many ships, including the battleships, from left,
the USS* West Virginia, *the USS* Tennessee, *and the USS* Arizona.

The Japanese aircraft dropped bombs on the ships,
causing huge explosions on impact. "Pearl Harbor was
a devastating sight," Hunter later wrote. "Very shortly,
the day became black as night. It was terrifying beyond
means of description."

Airmen from Ford Island Naval Station watch smoke and flames billow from the USS Shaw, *which had just been bombed by the Japanese.*

Hunter was witnessing a surprise attack by Japanese planes on the U.S. forces at Pearl Harbor. The attacks did not last very long. The first bombs struck at 7:55 that morning. By 10 o'clock, it was over. In that short period, the attackers took a terrible toll. Nearly 2,400 Americans died, and another 1,178 were wounded. Hospitals on the island of Oahu overflowed with victims of the attacks.

The Japanese planes crippled or destroyed much of the U.S. Pacific Fleet. They sank or badly damaged 21 ships stationed at Pearl Harbor, including eight enormous battleships. Almost 200 American planes were destroyed, and another 150 were damaged. Pearl Harbor was not the only U.S. military base attacked that day. Japanese forces also struck at bases in Hong Kong, Malay, Guam, the Philippines, and Wake Island.

The Japanese had hoped to deliver a crushing blow to American military forces in the Pacific. They very nearly succeeded. However, even the Japanese admiral who planned

A burned B-17 bomber sits at Hickam Field after the Japanese attack.

9

President Franklin D. Roosevelt signs the declaration of war.

the attacks worried that the surprise attack would backfire. "I fear we will awaken a sleeping giant," Admiral Isoroku Yamamoto said. He proved correct.

The day after the surprise attack, President Franklin D. Roosevelt asked Congress to declare war on Japan. Within a few days, the United States was also at war with Germany and Italy. The United States had entered World War II.

TWO NATIONS CLASH

The Japanese attack on Pearl Harbor followed years of bad relations between the United States and Japan. In the early years of the 20th century, Japan developed a powerful military. By the 1930s, its army and navy were the strongest in Asia, and its military leaders played a prominent role in the Japanese government.

Japan used its military might to gain new territory. In 1931, Japan invaded and easily conquered Manchuria. The United States protested this invasion, but Japan simply ignored the protest and continued its expansion. It took over parts of Korea and

Japanese soldiers marched into Manchuria in 1931. **11**

A terrified baby was one of the few people left alive after a Japanese attack on a Chinese train station in 1937.

the island of Formosa, now called Taiwan. In 1937, Japan launched an attack on China. In 1940, it invaded French Indochina, now called Vietnam. It established new military bases and colonies across Asia. Japan's new colonies provided food for its growing population and raw materials for its rapidly developing industries.

Japan's expansion worried some in the United States. Like Japan, the United States held military bases and controlled territories in the Pacific Ocean. As Japan continued to add more territory, a clash between the two countries began to seem more and more likely. The United States and other countries grew alarmed at Japan's acts of aggression. To punish Japan, the United States cut back on its trade with Japan. First, it stopped exporting aircraft and aircraft parts to Japan. Later, the U.S. established an **embargo** that stopped the sale of oil to Japan.

Japan's army and navy needed materials such as rubber and oil to keep its tanks, ships, and airplanes running. To get these raw materials, the Japanese military invaded countries that produced them. The Japanese set their sights on the Dutch East Indies, now called Indonesia, and other areas in the Pacific Ocean. The Japanese military hoped to control much of southeast Asia and the western part of the Pacific Ocean. Only one thing stood in its way: the United States military.

A worker taps a rubber tree in the Dutch East Indies in about 1940.

The United States had begun taking steps to stop the Japanese **war machine.** In 1941, the United States stationed 50 B-17 bomber planes in the Philippine Islands and stationed more ships at U.S. naval bases in the Pacific Ocean. These moves were designed to discourage the Japanese from beginning any new invasions.

Japan resented the U.S. efforts to stop its expansion. They saw the U.S. oil embargo and other actions as a threat to their national security. They demanded that the United States stop interfering in Japan's affairs. Diplomats from both countries met to discuss their differences, but the discussions accom-plished very little.

Secretary of State Cordell Hull (center) met with Japanese diplomats in 1941.

14

Germany's Adolf Hitler is greeted with the Nazi salute in the late 1930s.

Japan prepared for war. In 1940, Japan formed a three-way alliance with Adolf Hitler's Nazi Germany and with Italy. The three nations became known as the **Axis** partners. Like Japan, Germany aggressively sought to add new territory. As Axis powers, Germany, Japan, and Italy agreed to defend each other against attacks by other countries. By 1940, some leaders in the Japanese military were ready for war with the United States. They believed that their country's future depended on destroying the United States' power in the Pacific Ocean.

Hideki Tojo bows to Japanese Emperor Hirohito.

In October 1941, a general named Hideki Tojo became prime minister of Japan. As the head of Japan's government, he put his country on full alert for war. The rest of the world didn't know it yet, but a Japanese admiral had devised a plan to deliver a swift and punishing blow to the U.S. military.

PLANNING THE ATTACK

The plan to attack Pearl Harbor came from Admiral Isoroku Yamamoto. As commander in chief of Japan's navy, Yamamoto knew how important it was for Japan to have control of the oil fields of the Pacific Ocean. Without a steady supply of oil, the ships of Japan's powerful navy were useless. To gain control of the Pacific oil fields, Yamamoto believed Japan had to defeat the United States.

Yamamoto also knew the power of the United States. He had studied in the United States and understood well its size and economic strength. Yamamoto feared that war with the United States would end in disaster for Japan. He believed that

Isoroku Yamamoto

17

Crewmen prepare Japanese planes for attack on Pearl Harbor and Oahu.

in a long, drawn-out war, the United States would eventually wear Japan down. He believed Japan's only hope was to strike first and deliver a quick knockout blow to the U.S. military.

Yamamoto began considering a surprise attack on Pearl Harbor in 1940. Most other Japanese military planners believed that such an attack could never work. Pearl Harbor was 4,000 miles (6,400 kilometers) across the Pacific Ocean from Japan. How could Japanese ships and planes cross such a wide expanse of ocean without alarming U.S. forces?

Yamamoto insisted that it could be done, but it all depended on absolute secrecy and total surprise.

However, the United States knew Japan was planning some kind of attack. In 1940, U.S. Army **intelligence officers** cracked one of Japan's secret codes. This meant that the U.S military was able to understand coded messages that the Japanese government sent to its embassies in other countries. Based on the information gathered from such secret messages, the United States knew an attack was likely.

An American couple prepares to board a ferry for the first leg of their long trip home. They were among many people advised to leave Japan and China as tensions increased in late 1940.

Commanders of U.S. military posts in the Pacific Ocean were warned to expect a Japanese attack. "An aggressive move by Japan is expected within a few days," read one warning. The commanders at Pearl Harbor, General Walter Short and Admiral Husband Kimmel, received such warnings. The warnings

General Walter Short

did not say when or where the Japanese attack would occur, however. Even with the Japanese code solved, intelligence officers could not discover that information.

On December 7, U.S. Secretary of State Cordell Hull received a note from Japanese officials. "It is impossible to reach an agreement through further negotiations," the note read. Japan was breaking off peaceful discussions with the United States. Now it was clear that an attack would soon follow. Army Chief of Staff George C. Marshall sent a warning to bases in the Pacific Ocean to "be on the alert." By the time the warning reached Pearl Harbor, it was too late.

For months, Japanese forces planned and practiced in preparation for the attack on Pearl Harbor. The main Japanese attack force consisted of aircraft launched from ships called **aircraft carriers.** The aircraft carriers would sail to within about 230 miles (368 kilometers) of Hawaii. From there, the aircraft would fly to their targets at Pearl Harbor.

General George C. Marshall's warning came too late. **21**

The Japanese also planned to attack Pearl Harbor with midget submarines that carried just two crewmen and two **torpedoes.** Their mission was to make their way into Pearl Harbor undetected, then launch their torpedoes against the U.S. ships.

On November 26, a fleet of 31 warships and six aircraft carriers left Japan. They headed east, and by December 7, the fleet was in position, as planned, about 250 miles (400 kilometers) north of Hawaii. That morning,

Japanese pilots flew a fighter plane called the Zero.

The Japanese flag flies from the Mitsu, *which is in a long line of battleships in 1941.*

Japanese pilots gathered to pray in shrines aboard the aircraft carriers. Then they began taking off and flying toward their targets.

At Pearl Harbor, U.S. forces felt secure. Military commanders considered Pearl Harbor a natural fortress that would be difficult for enemy forces to attack. The naval base lay on the southern shore of the island of Oahu, one of eight islands that make up Hawaii. (At the time, Hawaii was a territory of the United States. It became a state in 1959.) The base could only be reached by a narrow waterway that was well defended. Scattered around the island were a number of other military bases, including airfields, naval stations, and **radar** sites. The Navy, Army, and Marine Corps all maintained posts on Oahu.

In Pearl Harbor itself sat more than 185 vessels of the U.S. fleet. The big battleships were lined up side by side on "Battleship Row." On the airfields of Oahu, aircraft sat side by side, too.

Commanders wanted to guard against **sabotage** attacks on the planes, so they ordered them stationed close together to make them easier to guard. Instead, this only made them easier targets for the attackers.

An aerial view of Pearl Harbor in December 1941

SURPRISE ATTACK

Just after daybreak on December 7, at 7:02 A.M., a radar station at Opana Point on Oahu received a signal that indicated a large group of planes approaching. Radar was new on the island and had only been used successfully elsewhere for a few months. Operators were not yet comfortable with the readings. Also, a large flight of American B-17 airplanes was due in from California about the same time, which added to the confusion of what the radar readings meant. In fact, the signals represented 183 Japanese planes. The first wave of attackers was about to hit Hawaii.

Earlier, at about 6:30 A.M., a U.S. ship spotted one of the small Japanese submarines trying to enter Pearl Harbor. It fired at the submarine and hit it. The U.S. forces still did not realize a large attack force was headed their way, however. So when planes began roaring over the rooftops of Oahu, many people figured they must be American planes.

25

A Japanese midget submarine missed its Pearl Harbor target and was found beached many miles away.

Then the Japanese torpedoes and bombs launched from the planes began hitting their targets. The attack was on.

The Japanese bombers flew in groups of five, working like teams to destroy targets one by one. Among the first **casualties** were 35 American servicemen at the Army's Hickam Air Field. They were eating breakfast when a Japanese plane sent a bomb toward their dining hall.

More than 1,100 of the people onboard the USS Arizona died in the attack.

Another plane dropped a 1,700-pound bomb on the USS *Arizona.* The bomb crashed through the ship's deck and into its **magazine,** where ammunition was stored. The explosion that followed was so enormous that some witnesses said the huge ship seemed to jump out of the water. A column of smoke and fire shot high into the sky. The explosion killed 1,177 of the *Arizona's* officers, sailors, and Marines.

Onboard the USS *Nevada,* the ship's band was just starting to play "The Star-Spangled Banner" during the daily flag-raising ceremony. Then the Japanese planes struck.

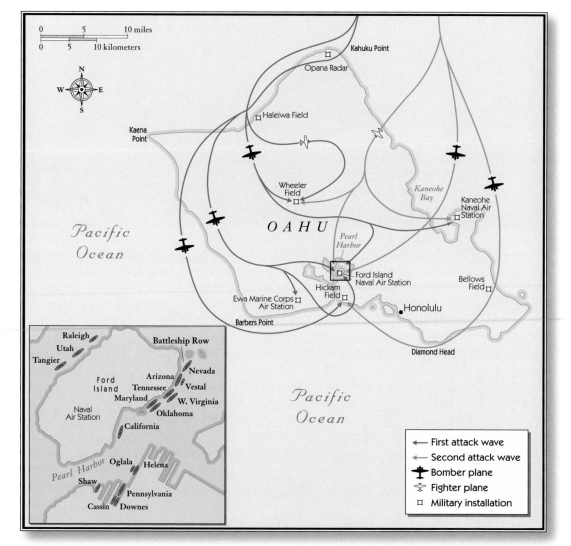

0   5   10 miles
0   5   10 kilometers

N
W · E
S

Kahuku Point

Opana Radar

Haleiwa Field

Kaena Point

Wheeler Field

Kaneohe Bay

Kaneohe Naval Air Station

Pacific Ocean

O A H U

Pearl Harbor

Ford Island Naval Air Station

Bellows Field

Hickam Field

Ewa Marine Corps Air Station

Honolulu

Barbers Point

Diamond Head

Pacific Ocean

Raleigh
Utah
Tangier

Battleship Row

Ford Island

Arizona   Nevada
Tennessee   Vestal
Maryland
W. Virginia
Oklahoma

Naval Air Station

California

Pearl Harbor Oglala   Helena

Shaw

Pennsylvania

Cassin   Downes

⟵ First attack wave
⟵ Second attack wave
✈ Bomber plane
✈ Fighter plane
◻ Military installation

A map shows the December 7, 1941, attack on Pearl Harbor.

The USS Nevada *burns in Pearl Harbor on the morning of the attack.*

The band continued to play through the attack until it finished its song. Sailors fired the ship's guns at the attacking planes and tried to steer the *Nevada* out of the harbor. The ship took several hits, however, and could not get away.

Torpedoes also hit the USS *Oklahoma*. The damage was so bad that the ship rolled and trapped more than 400 of its crewmen. Oil spilled in the water and caught

A Japanese pilot took this photo of a Japanese bomber heading toward burning U.S. ships.

fire, so that the harbor itself was burning. Many sailors trying
to swim to safety were badly burned.

About an hour after the attack began, a second wave
of Japanese aircraft arrived. They attacked four airfields
on Oahu and an army barracks. Some of the attacking
planes came in so low that American servicemen on the
ground could see the faces of the Japanese pilots.

Hundreds of American planes were destroyed before they could take off, and hundreds more servicemen were killed. A few U.S. pilots managed to take off and shoot down some Japanese aircraft, but the attacks kept coming. The Japanese lost just 29 aircraft and five small submarines on December 7.

A Japanese bomber pilot took this photo of a burning Wheeler Airfield on December 7.

31

By 10 o'clock that morning, the attack was over. In about two hours, the Japanese had crippled the U.S. Pacific Fleet and caused terrible casualties. One of the Japanese pilots sent a message back to his aircraft carrier: "Surprise Attack Successful."

The attack had not been a total success for the Japanese, however. They did not bomb the numerous oil storage tank farms around the harbor, so a ready supply of fuel was still available. They also missed the submarine pens, so U.S. submarines immediately set to sea to damage Japanese shipping.

The Japanese had hoped to destroy the American aircraft carriers based at Pearl Harbor. The aircraft carriers had been sent to other islands days earlier, so they were not at Pearl Harbor on December 7. They survived to join in the war that followed.

DECLARING WAR

In the hours after the attack on Pearl Harbor, survivors nervously watched the skies for more Japanese planes. A rumor spread that Japanese troops were parachuting onto the island of Oahu. According to another rumor, Japanese forces were attacking San Francisco, California. The rumors proved to be false.

Meanwhile, survivors worked to save servicemen who were wounded in the attacks or were trapped on

Female firefighters direct a hose to put out a blaze after the Japanese attack.

burning ships. On the USS *Utah,* rescuers followed tapping sounds and cut through the hull of the ship to rescue a sailor trapped inside.

DAILY NEWS FINAL

JAPAN AT WAR WITH U.S.
Hawaii, Philippines And Guam Bombed
FLEET HITS BACK

War news would dominate U.S. newspapers for the next four years.

Firefighters tried desperately to put out the many fires on the island and on ships in the harbor. Hospitals on Oahu overflowed with the wounded. In all, 1,178 men, women, and children were wounded in the attack.

News of Pearl Harbor reached President Franklin D. Roosevelt in Washington, D.C., on Sunday afternoon. Late that afternoon, the president learned that Japan had declared war on the United States. He began preparing the speech he would deliver to Congress asking for a declaration of war against Japan. The next day, Roosevelt spoke to Congress and to the nation.

34

"Yesterday, December 7, 1941—a date which will live in **infamy**—the United States was suddenly and deliberately attacked by naval and air forces of the Empire of Japan," Roosevelt said. "I ask that the Congress declare that since the unprovoked and dastardly attack by Japan on Sunday, December 7, a state of war has existed between the United States and the Japanese empire."

President Roosevelt spoke to Congress to ask for a declaration of war.

35

Less than an hour later, Congress declared war on Japan. On December 11, Germany and Italy declared war on the United States. That same day, the United States declared war on Germany and Italy.

Boys collected scrap metal as part of the U.S. war drive.

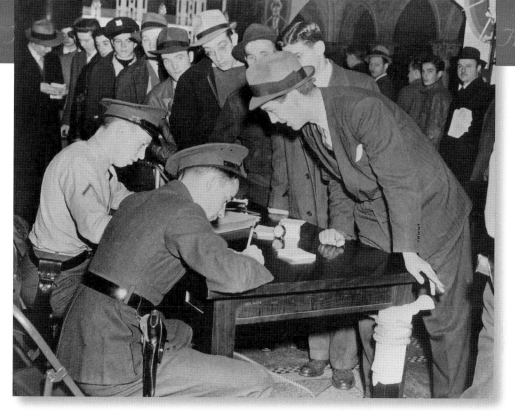

Long lines formed at military recruiting stations across the country in the days following the Pearl Harbor attack.

The American people responded to the United States' entry into the war. Before Pearl Harbor, public opinion had been divided over whether to get involved in World War II. Pearl Harbor changed that. Americans rallied to the war effort and resolved to defend the United States and defeat Japan and its Axis **allies**. Across the United States, young men lined up outside recruiting stations to join the Army, Navy, Marines, and Coast Guard.

In the months following Pearl Harbor, Japan was able to extend its control over the Pacific Ocean and Southeast Asia. Badly damaged by the attack at Pearl Harbor, U.S. forces could do little to stop them at first. Soon, however, Admiral Yamamoto's fears about U.S. industrial and military strength proved justified. It took four years and a great deal of suffering on all sides, but the United States did finally force Japan's surrender.

U.S. General Douglas MacArthur looked on as Shigemitsu Mamoru signed the Japanese surrender papers onboard the USS Missouri *on September 2, 1945.*

The formal surrender papers were signed onboard the USS *Missouri* in Tokyo Bay on September 2, 1945. In the harbor were many of the ships that had been damaged at Pearl Harbor.

Admiral Kimmel

Even before the war ended, the U.S. government began investigating why U.S. forces had been so completely surprised at Pearl Harbor. Government reports blamed the military commanders at Pearl Harbor for not properly preparing for attacks. Admiral Kimmel of the Navy and General Short of the Army were forced to resign from service.

39

PEARL HARBOR MEMORIAL

Signs of the terrible damage done on December 7 remained visible at Pearl Harbor throughout the war. The wreck of the USS *Arizona* came to rest in shallow water, so parts of the ship were still visible above the water. As they passed the *Arizona,* sailors on other ships saluted the mangled ship as a sign of respect to those who had lost their lives on December 7, 1941.

More than 1,000 crewmen of the USS Bennington *formed the word Arizona on their ship deck in a mass salute as they passed the sunken USS* Arizona *in 1958.*

Tourists pay their respects at the USS Arizona *Memorial, a National Park Service site in Pearl Harbor.*

After the war ended, plans were made to build a memorial on the spot where the *Arizona* sank. In 1961, construction was completed on a 184 foot (56 meter) structure over the remains of the ship. The memorial was dedicated the following year. The names of those killed on the *Arizona* are engraved on a marble wall in the memorial's shrine room. A plaque at the memorial reads, "Dedicated to the Eternal Memory of our gallant shipmates in the USS *Arizona* who gave their lives in action 7 December 1941."

The memorial has come to commemorate all the servicemen who were killed in the attack on Pearl Harbor.

41

GLOSSARY

aircraft carriers—ships with a special deck on which aircraft can land and take off

allies—countries that support one another in a conflict

Axis—the alliance of Germany, Italy, Japan, and other countries that opposed the Allies in World War II; the Allies were the United States, the Soviet Union, Great Britain, and France

battleships—ships outfitted with heavy armor and powerful guns

casualties—soldiers killed, wounded, captured or missing in battle

embargo—an act by a government stopping trade to or from another country

infamy—fame brought about by evil or shameful acts

intelligence officers—people in the military whose job is to gather secret information from other countries

magazine—a room aboard a ship where ammunition and explosives are stored

radar—an electronic device that uses radio waves to determine the location of an object such as a flying airplane

sabotage—to damage, destroy, or interfere with on purpose

torpedoes—missiles containing explosives that are launched from a tube in a submarine

war machine—the military forces of a country

42

DID YOU KNOW?

- Many of the U.S. ships damaged at Pearl Harbor were repaired and used by the Navy later in the war.

- "Remember Pearl Harbor" became a rallying cry for U.S. troops in the Pacific Ocean.

- Thousands of Japanese Americans served in the U.S. military during World War II.

- More than 1.4 million people visit the USS *Arizona* Memorial every year.

- A U.S. flag flies atop the memorial in Pearl Harbor. The memorial's flagpole is attached to the severed mast of the USS *Arizona* in tribute to the battleship and its lost crew.

IMPORTANT DATES

Timeline

1937	Japan invades China.
1940	September, Japan invades Indochina and forms an alliance with Italy and Germany; December, Admiral Isoroku Yamamoto begins planning an attack on Pearl Harbor.
1941	August, United States stops exporting oil to Japan; November 26, Japanese attack force leaves Japan and heads toward Pearl Harbor, Hawaii; December 7, Japanese attack Pearl Harbor; December 8, United States declares war on Japan.
1945	Japan formally surrenders on September 2.
1962	USS *Arizona* Memorial is dedicated in Pearl Harbor in May.

44

IMPORTANT PEOPLE

HUSBAND E. KIMMEL (1882–1968)

*Commander of naval forces at Pearl Harbor at the time of the
Japanese attack*

FRANKLIN D. ROOSEVELT (1882–1945)

*President of the United States who asked Congress to declare war on
Japan following the attack on Pearl Harbor*

WALTER C. SHORT (1880–1949)

Chief Army officer at Pearl Harbor at the time of the Japanese attack

HIDEKI TOJO (1884–1948)

*General and prime minister of Japan who prepared his country for
war with the United States*

ISOROKU YAMAMOTO (1884–1943)

Japanese admiral who planned the attacks on Pearl Harbor

WANT TO KNOW MORE?

At the Library

Allen, Thomas K. *Remember Pearl Harbor.* Washington, D.C.: National
Geographic, 2001.

Cooper, Michael. *Fighting for Honor: Japanese Americans and World War II.*
New York: Clarion, 2000.

Uschan, Michael V. *The Bombing of Pearl Harbor.* Milwaukee, Wis.:
World Almanac, 2003.

On the Web

For more information on *Pearl Harbor,* use FactHound

to track down Web sites related to this book.

1. Go to *www.facthound.com*

2. Type in a search word related to this book
   or this book ID: 0756506808.

3. Click on the *Fetch It* button.

Your trusty FactHound will fetch the best Web sites for you!

46

On the Road

USS Arizona Memorial

One Arizona Memorial Place

Honolulu, HI 96818

808/422-0561

To visit the memorial that honors those killed

in the 1941 attack on Pearl Harbor

San Diego Aerospace Museum

Balboa Park

2001 Pan American Plaza

San Diego, CA 92101

619/234-8291

To learn about the history of aviation and view World War II planes,

including a Japanese Zero

INDEX

About the Author

Andrew Santella writes for magazines and newspapers, including *GQ* and the *New York Times Book Review*. He is the author of a number of books for young readers. He lives outside Chicago with his wife and son.